INTRODUCTION

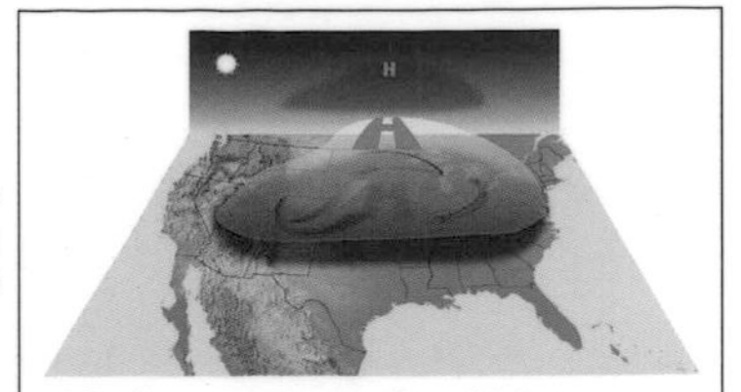

Heat waves occur when high pressure areas aloft trap heat near the ground.

Summer heat waves have become more frequent and increasingly intense over the past 20 years. In a normal year, about 175 Americans are killed by extreme heat. Among natural disasters, only extreme cold – not hurricanes, tornadoes, floods, or earthquakes – takes a greater toll. In the 40-year period from 1936 through 1975, nearly 20,000 people were killed in the United States by the effects of heat and solar radiation. In the disastrous heat wave of 1980, more than 1,250 people died. In the heat wave of 1995, more than 700 deaths in the Chicago area were attributed to heat.

Conditions that can compound heat-related health risks include stagnant atmospheric conditions and poor air quality. Consequently, people living in urban areas may be at greater risk from the effects of a prolonged heat wave than those living in rural areas. Also, asphalt and concrete store heat longer than soil and create an "urban heat island effect."

Preparation is Key

1. Know the Dangers
Learn about the relative risk of experiencing an extreme heat wave in your area. Contact your state emergency management office or local American Red Cross to learn more.

2. Learn Basic Survival Skills
Heat waves have predictable effects; typically power is knocked out as a result of increased use of cooling systems. As a result, people can be without light, refrigeration or air conditioning for days.

3. Don't Panic
Staying calm is the most important thing you can do in facing a survival situation. Excitement and alarm are natural emotions, but you must be able to manage them in order to make good decisions. Compose yourself and others and take charge of the situation.

4. Have an Action Plan
Personal safety, shelter and security are always your highest priority. Your first concern is to avoid injuries and stay safe until conditions return to normal.

- Determine the safest, coolest places to endure a heat wave at home and away.
- Prepare personal survival kits for every individual in your household, including pets.
- Have a plan to connect with friends and family during and after the heat wave so you can ensure everyone stays safe.

Waterford Press produces reference guides that introduce novices to nature, science, travel and languages. Product information and hundreds of educational games are featured on the website: **www.waterfordpress.com**

To order, call 800-434-2555. For permissions, or to share comments, e-mail editor@waterfordpress.com. For information on custom-published products, call 800-434-2555 or e-mail info@waterfordpress.com.

Scan for more info

Made in the USA

978-1-58355-859-1 $7.95 U.S
50795
ISBN 9 781583 558591
UPC 8 84682 01167 3

EXTREME HEAT SURVIVAL – PREPARE FOR & SURVIVE A HEAT WAVE

A DISASTER SURVIVAL GUIDE

EXTREME HEAT SURVIVAL

PREPARE FOR & SURVIVE A HEAT WAVE

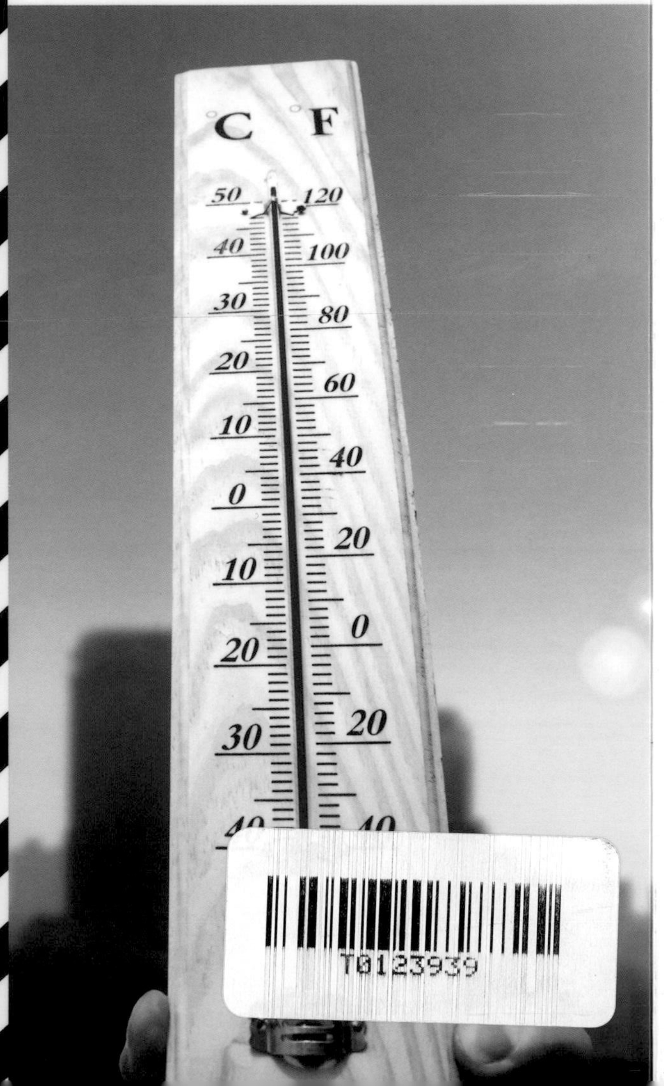

T0123939

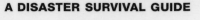

BEFORE – HOW TO PREPARE

There are specific terms used to designate extreme heat conditions:

Heat Wave - Prolonged period of excessive heat, often combined with excessive humidity.

Heat Index (HI) - A number in degrees tells how hot it feels when relative humidity is added to the air temperature. HI values were devised for shady, light wind conditions. Exposure to full sunshine can increase heat index values by up to 15°F (9°C). Also, strong winds, especially those with hot, dry air, can be extremely hazardous.

National Oceanic & Atmospheric Administration (NOAA) Heat Index

Temperature (*F)

Relative Humidity (%)	80	82	84	86	88	90	92	94	96	98	100	102	104	106	108	110
40	80	81	83	85	88	91	94	97	101	105	109	114	119	124	130	136
45	80	82	84	87	89	93	96	100	104	109	114	119	124	130	137	
50	81	83	85	88	91	95	99	103	108	113	118	124	131	137		
55	81	84	86	89	93	97	101	106	112	117	124	130	137			
60	82	84	88	91	95	100	105	110	116	123	129	137				
65	82	85	89	93	98	103	108	114	121	128	136					
70	83	86	90	95	100	105	112	119	126	134						
75	84	88	92	97	103	109	116	124	132							
80	84	89	94	100	106	113	121	129								
85	85	90	96	102	110	117	126	135								
90	86	91	98	105	113	122	131									
95	86	93	100	108	117	127										
100	87	95	103	112	121	132										

Likelihood of Heat Disorders with Prolonged Exposure or Strenuous Activity

Caution · Extreme Caution · Danger · Extreme Danger

Heat Index and Potential Health Disorders

Heat Index 90°-105°F – Heat cramps, heat exhaustion and heat stroke possible with continued exposure and/or continued physical activity.

Heat Index 105°-130°F – Heat cramps and heat exhaustion likely, heat stroke possible with continued exposure and/or continued physical activity.

Heat Index 130°F or higher – Heat exhaustion and heat stroke likely with continued exposure and/or continued physical activity.

Prepare Your Home

- Cover windows that let in sunlight with drapes or shades, or tape aluminum foil on them to reflect heat outside.
- Maintain cooling equipment by having it cleaned and inspected annually. Ensure air conditioning ducts are properly insulated, and that all window units are sealed airtight.
- Back up your main cooling system with a portable air conditioner that can be run by a generator should the power fail.
- Weatherstrip doors and windows to keep the heat out. Install storm windows or cover windows with plastic to add an additional layer of insulation from the heat.
- House fires pose an additional risk during heat waves. Keep fire extinguishers on hand, and make sure everyone in your house knows how to use them.
- Fill your freezers full of ice and turn it up to maximum cold. In the event of a power failure, you'll have temporary refrigeration for perishable foods and a source of water after the ice melts.

BEFORE – WHAT TO EXPECT

System Failures

Power Failure

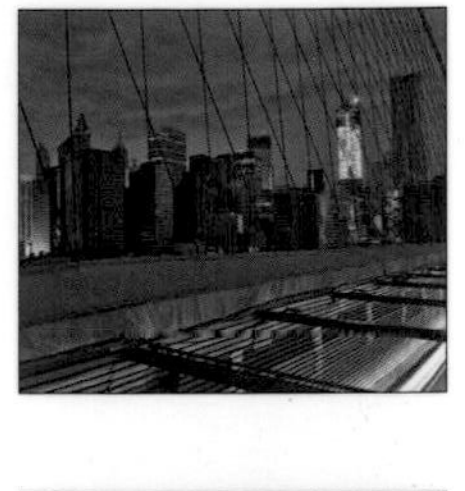

Systems can crash as a result of the demand from high use of air conditioners. Blackouts can cause businesses to shut down, elevators to stop running and hospitals to be evacuated. It may take days or weeks for power to return.

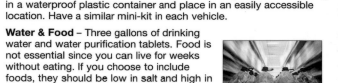

Personal Risks

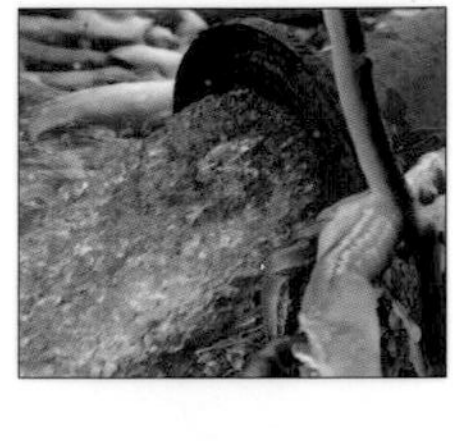

Extreme heat combined with stagnant air traps pollutants and creates poor air-quality conditions in big cities. Further health risks are created when prolonged power loss creates unsanitary conditions and health resources become further strained.

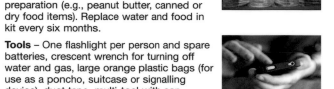

Injury/Illness

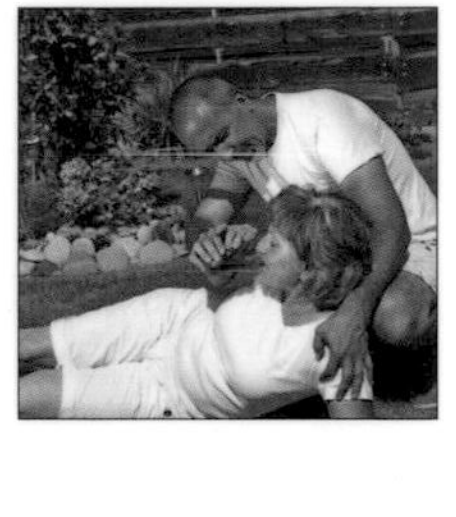

Heat cramps and heat exhaustion can precede heat stroke, which is a life-threatening condition. It is critical that people suffering from heat stress can be cooled down before their condition worsens. The most vulnerable people in extreme heat are the elderly (especially those over 75), babies/young children, people with heart, breathing, or mobility problems, those suffering from mental illnesses and those that have to be active outside (e.g., athletes, laborers).

Looting/Theft

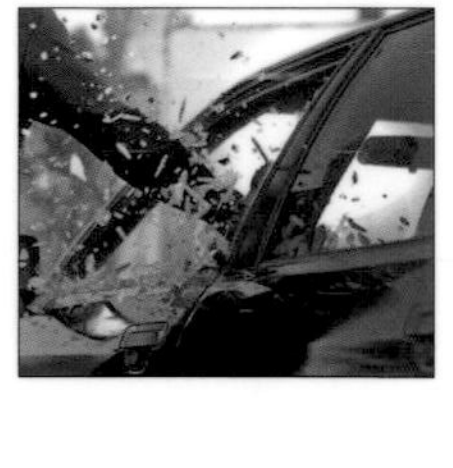

People who are unprepared may panic and steal possessions from stores, households and individuals to survive. Have some form of defense – pepper spray or a weapon – to protect you and your family from harm.

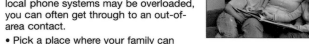

Isolation/Restricted Movement

Power failures strand people without air conditioning, light, refrigeration, and limit the ability to travel using mass transit in large cities.

Heat Wave Alerts

The National Weather Service uses specific terms and definitions that communicate the severity of the impending heat wave:

Excessive Heat Outlook – Issued when the potential exists for an excessive heat event in the next 3-7 days.

Excessive Heat Watch – Issued when conditions indicate an excessive heat event in the next 24 to 72 hours.

Excessive Heat Warning – Issued when an excessive heat event is expected in the next 36 hours.

Scan for more info

National Weather Service

BEFORE – CREATE AN ACTION PLAN

What to Do Before a Heat Wave Occurs

- Listen to weather stations for status updates.
- Prepare an emergency survival kit.
- Fill bathtubs and all available containers with water in case you are cut off from services.

1. Determine the Safest Place to Endure the Event

Pick a place at home and away where you and your family can shelter during the heat wave. The safest place is usually the most structurally sound part of a building on the lowest floor. Be prepared to evacuate if local authorities announce a directive to evacuate. If you are not required to evacuate, plan to stay indoors and away from windows.

2. Learn About Your Local Support Network

When a heat wave strikes, survival can depend on a few basic elements. Having access to clean water and a shelter that provides protection from the elements and sanitation in the days and weeks after a disaster event are critical.

- Learn which public buildings such as libraries, schools, malls and shelters are likely to provide a cool sanctuary during the hottest parts of the day.
- Arrange temporary housing at a friend or relative's home outside the threatened area in case you need to evacuate.
- People with disabilities require special consideration. Be sure to establish a network of family or friends to assist you in moving a disabled person in an emergency. Learn how to operate a wheelchair if necessary. Ensure you have all the supplies they may need, including batteries for hearing aids, current prescriptions and dosages, names and addresses of doctors and pharmacists and detailed information about their medical regimen. Learn the location of more than one facility that provides any life-saving service, including dialysis.

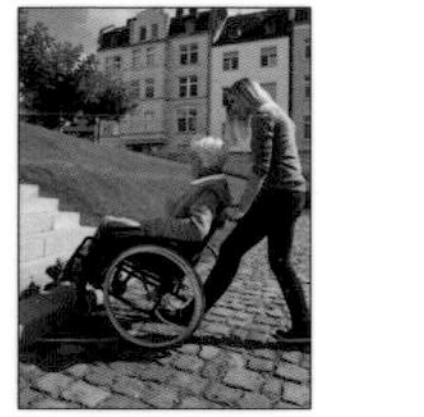

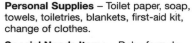

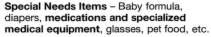

- FEMA recommends for each pet you'll need an animal crate, leash, collar with ID and food, water and medications to last several days. If you need to move to a shelter, ensure it is pet-friendly before you go.

3. Make a Family Action Plan

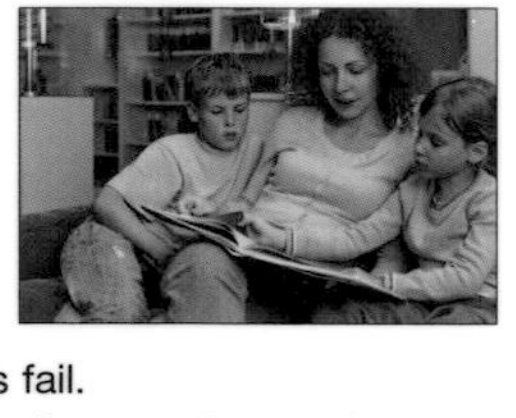

- Create a card of key contacts for each family member. Have a designated contact out of the immediate area. While local phone systems may be overloaded, you can often get through to an out-of-area contact.
- Pick a place where your family can meet should the heat wave should systems fail.
- Let relatives or friends know the location of your safe room/area and meeting points.

4. Practice Response

Plan safe places and escape routes in and around your home, office and school. Practice retreating to safe areas with your family members at least twice a year. Find and rehearse steps to get to your safe places from various locations. Learn emergency first aid and CPR to be able to help others if needed.

BEFORE – PREPARE SURVIVAL KITS

5. Prepare a Personal Survival Kit for Each Individual

Each kit should sustain an individual for three days. Put the following in a waterproof plastic container and place in an easily accessible location. Have a similar mini-kit in each vehicle.

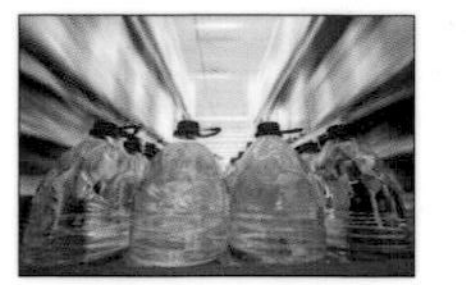

Water & Food – Three gallons of drinking water and water purification tablets. Food is not essential since you can live for weeks without eating. If you choose to include foods, they should be low in salt and high in calories and require no refrigeration or preparation (e.g., peanut butter, canned or dry food items). Replace water and food in kit every six months.

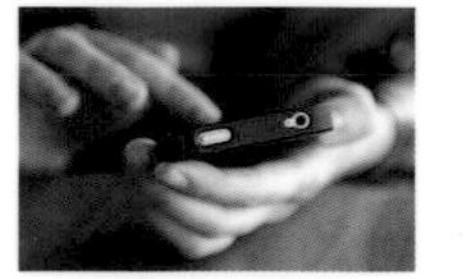

Tools – One flashlight per person and spare batteries, crescent wrench for turning off water and gas, large orange plastic bags (for use as a poncho, suitcase or signalling device), duct tape, multi-tool with can opener, three sources of fire (e.g., lighter, matches, flint), candles, pens, paper, 50 ft. of rope and a signal whistle.

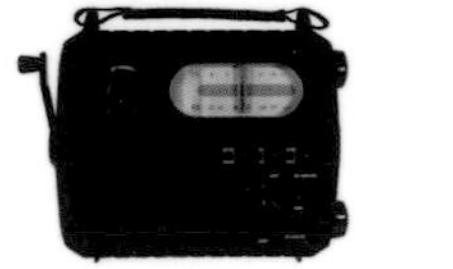

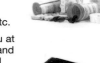

Communications – Battery- or crank-operated radio/flashlight or TV, cellphones and spare batteries. Many crank radios can also charge cellphones.

Personal Supplies – Toilet paper, soap, towels, toiletries, blankets, first-aid kit, change of clothes.

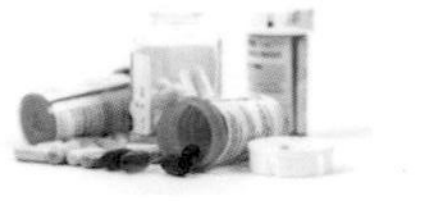

Special Needs Items – Baby formula, diapers, **medications and specialized medical equipment**, glasses, pet food, etc.

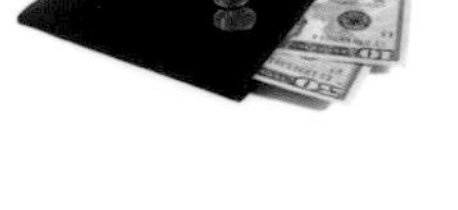

Paperwork – Identification (carry with you at all times). Contact info for family, friends and emergency services, cash (small bills) and credit cards, copies of insurance papers, mortgage, bank accounts, proof of occupancy (utility bill). Keep paperwork in a separate waterproof container.

Security – Pepper spray or a weapon to fend off aggressive animals and bad people.

Survival Bucket Strategy

A simple way to prepare for disasters is to use the survival bucket strategy. Simply put, every member of a household – including pets – should have a sturdy five gallon bucket with a lid that contains enough supplies for them to survive 3 DAYS without water or power. Fill it with your survival gear (excluding phones, medications and paperwork), seal it, label it and store it where it is easy to find. Add the missing items at the last minute. A bucket is the ideal storage device because it is waterproof and also has many additional uses including stool/table, flotation device, wash basin, solar still, noisemaker for signal, water heater, bailing tool, toilet and shovel.

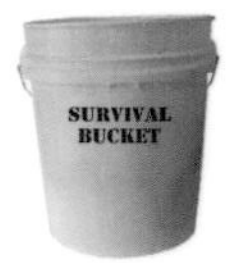

Scan this code to purchase survival bucket supplies online.

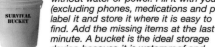

Bring all pets inside and move other animals and livestock into sheltered areas. **Get indoors and stay there until the heat wave passes.** Limit exposure to direct sunlight, limit physical activity, stay hydrated.

ONCE YOU ARE INDOORS

• Take shelter in an interior room on the lowest floor of the building away from windows, doors and outside walls that will be a source of heat. Close off air conditioning to other rooms. Seal the edges of doors from the inside with tape, plastic or hang blankets to limit hot air from entering, but do not create an air tight environment that might cause suffocation.

• Keep your room at a comfortable – not cold – temperature in order to conserve energy. Use air conditioners at low-usage times (like the late evening, nighttime and early morning) to avoid over-stressing the power grid. If the power goes off, turn off all electrical breakers and disconnect all electrical appliances.

• Dress in loose-fitting, lightweight clothes, turn on fans and wet down clothing to stay cool. Have cool baths and showers.

• Eat well-balanced, light, and regular meals. Foods dense in calories like meats and cheeses take more metabolic energy to break down and increase water loss.

• Avoid using salt tablets unless directed to do so by a physician.

• Drink plenty of water; even if you do not feel thirsty. Avoid drinks with caffeine or alcohol that will dehydrate you.

• Check on your animals frequently to ensure that they are not suffering from the heat and have adequate shade and water.

• Consider spending the warmest part of the day in public buildings such as libraries, schools, movie theaters, shopping malls, and other community facilities.

IF YOU MUST GO OUTSIDE

• Dress in loose-fitting, lightweight clothes that cover as much skin as possible. The ideal outfit is one with an outer layer of lightweight white clothing (to reflect sunlight) over an inner layer of lightweight dark clothing (to block ultraviolet light and prevent moisture from evaporating).

• Protect face and head from the direct sun by wearing a wide-brimmed hat or using an umbrella when outside. Ideally, you should do any traveling at dusk, dawn or during the night.

• Avoid strenuous work during the warmest part of the day. Use a buddy system when working in extreme heat, and take frequent breaks if you must work outside.

IF YOU ARE STRANDED IN A VEHICLE

A vehicle without air-conditioning acts like an oven in direct sunlight. In this situation, the key to survival is finding shade and remaining near your vehicle since this will be easier to spot by rescuers. If no shade is available, lie in the shadow of, or under, your vehicle. If possible, dig down into the earth where the soil will be cooler.

Major Health Risks During Extreme Heat

Prolonged exposure to intense heat causes the body's core heat to rise, resulting in cramps, exhaustion, heat stroke and eventually, death. When in doubt, seek medical attention.

Sunburn

Symptoms: Redness and pain from exposure to the sun. In severe cases, swelling of skin, blisters, fever and headaches.

First Aid: Get victim out of the sun, lay them down and apply cool, wet cloths. If blisters break, cover them with a sterile, dry cloth (do not apply ointments).

Heat Cramps

Symptoms: Painful cramps and spasms, usually in muscles of the legs or abdomen.

First Aid: Apply firm pressure on cramping muscles, or gently massage to relieve spasm. Give sips of water. If nausea occurs, discontinue treatment and seek medical attention.

Heat Exhaustion

Symptoms: Heavy sweating, weakness, skin cold, pale and clammy, pulse weak, possible fainting and vomiting. Normal temperature is possible. Typically occurs when people exercise heavily or work in a hot, humid place where body fluids are lost through heavy sweating. Blood flow to the skin increases, causing blood flow to decrease to the vital organs. This results in a form of mild shock. If not treated, the victim's condition will worsen.

First Aid: Get victim into a cool, shaded area. Lay down and loosen clothing. Apply cool, wet cloths. Fan or move victim to an air conditioned room. Administer sips of cool water. If vomiting occurs, discontinue and seek medical attention immediately.

Heat Stroke (Sunstroke, Hyperthermia)

Symptoms: Altered mental state, confusion, nausea, dizziness, throbbing headache, hot dry skin, rapid and strong pulse, possible unconsciousness. High body temperature – 104° F (40° C) or higher. This life-threatening condition occurs when the victim's internal cooling system stops working. The body temperature can rise so high that brain damage and death may result if the body is not cooled quickly.

First Aid: HEAT STROKE IS A SEVERE MEDICAL EMERGENCY. SUMMON EMERGENCY MEDICAL ASSISTANCE OR GET THE VICTIM TO A HOSPITAL IMMEDIATELY. Move the victim to a cool, shaded or air-conditioned space, remove excess clothing and cool their body with wet towels and fans until the ambulance arrives. Ideally, immerse victim in an ice bath. Do not give fluids.

Each year, dozens of children and untold numbers of pets left in parked vehicles die from heat stoke. The temperature inside a parked vehicle can rapidly rise to a dangerous level for children, pets and even adults in a matter of minutes. Leaving the windows open does not significantly decrease the temperature inside the vehicle. For this reason, **NEVER** leave a child or pet unattended in a vehicle.

---

1. Is Your Location Still Safe and Secure?

If your safe area becomes compromised – for example, a power failure causes air conditioners and refrigerators to shut down, which causes the temperature inside the building to rise to unsafe levels – take your survival kits and move everyone to a designated public shelter. **Text SHELTER + your ZIP code to 43362 (4FEMA)** to find the nearest shelter in your area (example: shelter 12345).

Scan for more info

FEMA

2. Is Anyone Injured or Trapped?

Help injured or trapped persons. Check on neighbors who may require special assistance with infants, the elderly and people with accessibility and medical/functional needs.

• Assess and treat any minor injuries as you are qualified and able to do so. To treat sunburns and other burns, remove any jewelry and flush the burned area with cold water until pain subsides. DO NOT touch or clean burned area, pop blisters or apply ointments or sprays to the burn. Cover the area with a dry, sterile cloth.

• Do not attempt to move seriously injured people unless they are in immediate danger of further injury. Get medical assistance immediately. If someone has stopped breathing, begin CPR.

3. Making Contact With Others

Contact family members and friends to ensure they do not need assistance. If you or a member of your family become separated or goes missing, DO NOT CALL THE POLICE; they will be overwhelmed with other demands. Instead, contact the American Red Cross at 1-800-RED-CROSS/1-800-733-2767.

Scan for more info

Red Cross

4. Moving Around After a Heat Wave

After an extreme heat wave, minimize travel to avoid overexposure to the heat.

• When outside, protect yourself from the direct sun by wearing lightweight, loose-fitting, long-sleeved shirts and pants, and carry an umbrella or wear a wide-brimmed hat to protect your head.

• Be careful what you touch. Metal objects can be extremely hot and cause second-degree burns when touched.

• Always carry water and keep your clothing wet to facilitate cooling.

• Drive only if it is absolutely necessary.

• Avoid overexertion since this can trigger a heart attack.

General Safety Considerations

• Continue to monitor your cellphone, radio or television for emergency information.

• If you are away from home, do not return until authorities say it is safe to do so.

• If you suspect any damage to your home, shut off electrical power, natural gas and propane tanks to avoid fire, electrocution or explosions.

• Do not use tap water unless you are certain it is safe; cracks in pipes can cause inadvertent flooding and risk of contamination.

• For insurance purposes, take pictures of any damages.

Survival Priorities

Statistically speaking, the most likely causes of death during a disaster are becoming too cold (hypothermia) or too hot (hyperthermia). Depending on where you live – Anchorage vs. Phoenix – your survival strategy and the contents of your survival kit should be adapted to suit your environment.

Shelter

Protection from the elements will allow you to preserve strength and restore energy. If your safe area becomes compromised during the event, either repair the damages or move to another shelter.

1. Stay as hydrated as possible; limit exertion.

2. Protect yourself from the elements; stay out of the sun and wind.

3. Stay on the lowest floor of your house, where it is coolest. If outdoors, seek the safest source of shade and build your shelter around/under that. If there is ample fresh water available, wet your clothes to increase cooling.

Water

You can only survive 3 days without water, and even less in hot, arid surroundings. Carefully ration the fresh water you have for drinking only (one gallon per person per day under normal conditions). Never waste water; after use for cooking and bathing, it can be used as gray water for other purposes.

Drinking Water

Can be obtained from several sources. In addition to the water stored in tub(s) and sinks, sources of fresh water inside a building include:

Water pipes – Once you shut off the water to a building, the water pipes remain full of water. Turn off your hot water heater and water treatment system and drain the water from the pipes via taps into food-quality containers.

Hot water heater – The hot water heater in most homes contains 20-30 gallons of water. Simply drain from the faucet at the bottom.

Toilet tanks – Each holds 2-4 gallons. Purify before drinking.

Hot water heater

Heat Wave Duration Increase
January–May 2012

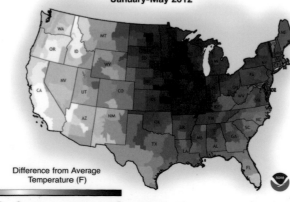

Difference from Average Temperature (F)

-2   0   8

Gray Water

Use gray water from streams, ponds and puddles for uses other than drinking. Most gray water can be purified for drinking if needed.

To flush a toilet, fill a bucket with one gallon of gray water. Pour the water into the toilet bowl in one thrust, fast enough to push the contents of the bowl down the drain. If the sewage system is damaged, do not flush toilets or drain sinks as it may trigger a "backwash" that would further damage your home.

How to Purify Water

If the water system fails, NEVER drink tap water unless you are certain it is not contaminated. To be safe, water should always be purified before drinking.

Three simple ways to purify water are:

1. Bring water to a rolling boil for 10 minutes;

2. Treat with purification tablets, iodine (12 drops per gallon) or bleach (1/2 tablespoon per gallon);

3. Use a water pump or gravity-fed purifier to strain bacteria from the water.

Fire

With fire/heat you can purify water, cook or preserve food and signal for rescue.

• Your survival kit should have at least three types of fire starter.

• Your barbecue, camping stove or gas lanterns are a potential source of heat that can be used to heat and purify water and cook foods. Never use indoors; carbon monoxide released from these burning gases will kill you.

• Portable generators can provide temporary power to key sources like the refrigerator and air conditioning units. Ensure you have enough gas to keep it running sporadically for several days and never run indoors.

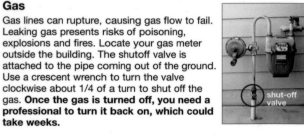

The Silent Killer

Never use generators, grills, camp stoves or other gasoline, propane, natural gas or charcoal-burning devices inside your home, garage or camper. Carbon monoxide (CO) – an odorless, colorless gas that is given off when these fuels are burned – can cause sudden illness and death if you breathe it. If you suspect CO poisoning and are feeling dizzy, light-headed or nauseated, get into fresh air and seek medical help immediately. Even burning candles in an airtight room can cause asphyxiation and death.

Locate the main shutoff valves to your home or building before you are faced with an emergency. **Listen carefully to news reports that will inform you when to turn off your utilities.**

Power

Shut off electricity to the house to avoid power surges that can cause fires. Locate the power breaker box. If you have circuit breakers, there is usually a double breaker at the top of the row of breakers marked 'Main'. Flip that one and it shuts the house power off. Otherwise, simply turn off each individual breaker. Disconnect electrical appliances.

Water

To turn off the water to the building, locate the main shut-off valve (usually under a metal plate near the street at the front of the building). Lift off the plate and use a crescent wrench to turn the valve clockwise about 1/4 of a turn to shut the water off. In many homes, a secondary shut-off valve is located in the garage or basement. If the building is on a well, find out where the shut-off valve is.

Crescent Wrench

Gas

Gas lines can rupture, causing gas flow to fail. Leaking gas presents risks of poisoning, explosions and fires. Locate your gas meter outside the building. The shutoff valve is attached to the pipe coming out of the ground. Use a crescent wrench to turn the valve clockwise about 1/4 of a turn to shut off the gas. **Once the gas is turned off, you need a professional to turn it back on, which could take weeks.**

Emergency Etiquette

• Cooperate fully with public safety officials. If asked to relocate, do so immediately. Failure to relocate when asked creates an unfair load on emergency response personnel to find or rescue you, instead of on the community-wide recovery operations that will help everyone get back home as quickly and safely as possible.

• Only use your telephone for urgent calls to avoid tying up the available airspace.

• Keep your children and animals under your direct control.

• Report failures in power, water and gas to local utilities.

• Respond to requests for volunteer assistance by police, fire fighters and relief organizations, but **do not provide assistance unless assistance has been requested.**

• If you are going to a community shelter, bring your emergency supplies. Your stay will be more comfortable if you have your own food, water, clothes, sleeping bags and some activities (books, cards, etc.) with which to pass the time. Access to power sources will be limited, so take extra batteries for your communications devices.